Recipes from Lakeland

collected by readers
of *Cumbria* magazine

Dalesman Books 1989

The Dalesman Publishing Company Ltd.,
Clapham, via Lancaster, LA2 8EB.

© Dalesman Publishing Company Ltd 1989

ISBN: 0 85206 975 8

Printed by Peter Fretwell & Sons Ltd.,
Goulbourne Street, Keighley, West Yorkshire BD21 1PZ.

CONTENTS

Drawings in the text by Valary Gustard, Victoria Wright and Barbara Yates.

Oven Settings

Some of the recipes in ths book use traditional
descriptions for oven settings. The conversion factors
for electric and gas ovens are as follows:-

	Electric	Gas
Very Slow	250	1
Slow	300	2
Moderate	350	4
Hot (or Quick)	400	6
Very Hot	475	8

Lakeland Cooking

PLAIN, simple and very wholesome: these are the hallmarks of cooking, Lakeland style. Many people have drawn up chairs to enjoy high tea when there did not appear to be too much on the table, only to discover that the cakes and scones and pies were made with such substantial ingredients that there was still plenty left when their appetites had been satisfied.

Mrs Beeton remarked that the inhabitants of Cumberland and Westmorland were noted for their pies and puddings. The traditional dishes of this region are mainly of a substantial nature, well suited to the appetites of a largely agricultural population living in an area where the air is often as tingling fresh as wine brought straight up from the cellar.

There was a time when the menu was not very extensive. On the dale farms, up to and beyond the time of William Wordsworth, families tucked in to beef and mutton. The mutton came from Herdwicks, the native sheep. Surplus stock was killed off in autumn, to be cured and preserved for use during the coming year. As a change from well-salted meat, the local people could rely on fresh fish: salmon moving up the lakes and rivers to spawn, the native brown trout, and toothsome char, inhabiting the deeper parts of the lakes.

Visitors to the Lakes looked forward to sitting down in front of a char pie at one of the leading hotels. Old-time writers like Camden, Pennant and Gray noted that the char was a table delicacy. There were three ways of dealing with this fish, which Camden referred to as "a sort of golden 'alpine' trout". It could be made into pies, some of them enormous creations. Char could be potted, or eaten freshly caught.

In the old "statesman" days a great deal of home-brewed ale was drunk, and each farm yielded milk, handily converted into butter and cheese. Lowland Cumberland was always a notable area for producing grain. Tea and coffee came into the lives of the folk of the remote dales about the time of William Wordsworth.

A staple food was oatmeal, either very moist as porridge (or "poddish"), or crisp and dry as oatcake, cooked on the

5

"backstones" of farms and cottages. Oatmeal was used for pie-crusts and gingerbread, like the Kendal "piggin bottoms" which were snaps stamped out of rolled dough by the iron rim forming the base of a "piggin", or small wooden tub.

*   *   *

The Lake Counties have had their wigs. Hawkshead has had a special association with them. One recipe, dated 1710, gives the ingredients as a quarter peck of fine flour; 3lb of butter, rubbed in fine; ½lb of sugar; half a nutmeg, half a race of ginger; three eggs. "Beat well, and put to half a pint of yeast and three spoonsful of sack," states the recipe, with terms that mean little to a modern housewife. "Make a hole in the flour and pour in, with as much milk (just warm) as will make it into a light paste. Let it stand before the fire to rise half an hour. Then make one dozen and a half wigs, and brush them over with egg. Put into a quick oven and bake for half an hour."

Kendal Mint Cake, another old-timer, is now produced in large quantities by commercial concerns, and it is a source of quiet Cumbrian pride that some of was carried up Everest by the British expedition that made the first ever ascent of the world's highest peak.

For mint cake you want: 1lb sugar; ¼ pint of milk; ½ teaspoon or three drops of peppermint essence. You put the sugar and milk into a pan, and boil it until it forms a soft ball. Remove from the heat, and add the essence. Now beat the mixture well until it is smooth and slightly setting, but still liquid. Pour into a buttered tin, but keep back one tablespoonful, beaten until it grains. Add this to the top of the mint cake when it is in the tin.

*   *   *

Grasmere, at the heart of the Wordsworth country, has its distinctive shortbread and gingerbread. Cumbrians have for years added rum to butter. The housewives at farms and cottages have for long made a speciality of baking cakes.

You'll find nothing really fancy in the old-style fare of the Lake District, but you can guarantee that it is wholesome and satisfying. In this book are some recipes which, while not distinctively of this region, have found a place in its kitchen literature. Most of them have been contributed by readers of *Cumbria*. We thank them for their interest and help. Through their generosity many fine recipes are now shared with people living in all parts of the land.

SOUPS

Butter Bean Soup

½lb butter beans
1 onion
2 carrots
1 slice turnip
1oz butter
1 dessertspoon flour

1 stalk celery
2 potatoes
2 or 3 tomatoes
1 quart water or stock
½ pint milk
salt and pepper to taste

Steep the beans in boiling water overnight, remove skins, place in pan with water or stock, add grated onion, turnip, carrot, celery and potatoes, simmer two hours; rub through a fine sieve. Return to clean saucepan, add the butter, pepper and salt, and flour, mixed to a smooth paste with milk, place the tomatoes in boiling water for two minutes and remove skins. Then slice and add to soup; simmer slowly for about ten minutes until tomatoes dissolve. Serve with toast.

Cream of Potato Soup

1 or 2 cups chopped cooked boiled or steamed potatoes
2 cups potato water
3 cups hot milk
salt and pepper to taste
1½oz butter

1½oz flour
1 small onion, chopped finely
1 teaspoon chopped parsley

Place the potatoes in a saucepan. Add potato water and chopped onion and parsley. Cover and simmer for 20 minutes. Melt butter in another pan. Stir in flour, off the heat, and when smooth, stir in hot milk by degrees. Return to heat and stir till boiling. Add the potato broth which may be whisked or sieved. Season to taste with salt and pepper. Add parsley. Enough for 4 to 6 persons. NOTE—Boiled and sieved turnip may be added if desired.

Mutton Broth

1lb mutton (neck) or 1lb beef (flat ribs)

1 tablespoon barley	pepper to taste
small piece cabbage	2 teaspoons parsley
1 carrot	1 onion
1 small turnip	¼pt dried peas (soaked overnight)
2 teaspoons salt	3 pints water

Chop up all vegetables. Wash barley and tie meat into nice shape, put them into a pan with water to simmer slowly. Cook for about half an hour, add vegetables, boil all together for one and a half hours, skimming frequently. Season with salt and pepper and add chopped parsley. Place meat on a hot dish and serve separately, with a little of the liquid poured over it.

Game Soup

The remains of any cold game
2 medium sized carrots
1 bay leaf
2 peppercorns
2oz finely chopped liver
1 wine glass sherry to every quart of stock
1 large onion
1 bunch mixed herbs (quantity and mixture to taste)
2 or 3 cloves
the whites of 2 eggs
1 teaspoon brown sugar
poultry stock or water

Put the game into a pan with the chopped liver, onion, carrots, herbs, bay leaf, peppercorns, cloves and sugar. Cover with stock or water and bring to the boil. Simmer for one hour, then strain and when cold add the egg whites lightly beaten, and a wineglass of sherry to every quart of stock and whisk all well together. Put the game meat, cut into small pieces, back into the soup, thicken as desired, return to the pan and bring to the boil.

FISH DISHES

Fish Mulligan

3 strips bacon, diced
3 onions, sliced and peeled
1½lb cod or haddock fillets
1½lb potatoes, pared and cubed
½ teaspoon celery seed
3 large carrots, pared and cubed
¼ cup green pepper, diced
1½ teaspoons salt
¼ teaspoon pepper
3 cups boiling water
1 large can tomatoes (3½ cups)
2 tablespoons mixed parsley

Brown bacon lightly in a deep pot. Remove bacon and set aside. Brown onions in bacon fat until golden. Cut fish into 2-inch pieces and add with potatoes, celery seed, carrots, green peppers, salt and pepper. Add boiling water and simmer, covered till vegetables are tender. (About 20 minutes). Add tomatoes and heat, do not boil. Garnish with parsley and the bacon.

Salmon Scouse

Quantity will depend on number to be served. Fresh salmon, steamed and skin and bones removed (or tin of grade 1 salmon). Mix into smoothly mashed potatoes. Serve with egg sauce (hard boiled eggs chopped into white sauce).

Creamed Fish with Potato Border

1lb cooked sieved potatoes   3/4 pint white sauce
1lb fresh haddock   2 eggs
1/2oz butter   2oz grated cheese

Steam and mash the potatoes. Add eggs and butter. Beat and season to taste. Shape with floured hands into a round border in a buttered fireproof dish and ornament with a fork. Bake in a moderate oven until brown. Meanwhile, boil, drain and flake haddock into white sauce. Stir in grated cheese. Season to taste. Stir till cheese is melted. Pour into the border. Sprinkle fish with chopped parsley.

Potted Char (the Char is a Windermere fish)

Clean and scale the fish and cook it slowly in white wine with a few slices of onion and carrot and pieces of parsley stalk. Allow to cool, skin it, and remove the fillets. Be careful to take out all bones. Now arrange the fillets or pieces of fillet in an earthenware pot and cover them with melted butter. Place the pot, with contents covered, in a moderate oven for 20 to 30 minutes, and on withdrawing add more clarified butter if required. (Fillets must be covered with butter). Will keep for some time in a cool place.

Scalloped Fish

2 cups sieved boiled or steamed potato
2 cups steamed white fish
1 1/2 cups well-seasoned white sauce
1/2 cup stale crumbs
1 tablespoon chopped chives
2 tablespoons melted butter
pepper and salt to taste; paprika to taste

Add paprika, chives and pepper and salt to taste to the potato. Line a shallow buttered fireproof dish thinly with the mixture. Add a layer of flaked fish, then half the sauce. Cover with remainder of potato, then with remainder of sauce. Sprinkle with crumbs, then with butter. Bake in a moderate oven for 25 minutes.

MEAT AND POULTRY

Lakeland Hot-Pot

2lbs neck of mutton
2 carrots, sliced
3 medium sized onions, sliced
salt and pepper
water
2lbs potatoes, sliced and peeled
3 small black puddings, cut in half

Place all the ingredients in a stew pot, arranging a layer of the
potatoes last. Season to taste and add sufficient water to cover.
Cook for about 3 hours in a moderate oven. Remove the lid to
brown the potatoes and serve piping hot.

Westmorland Farm House Pie

1½lb fresh beef
1lb mutton
2 rashers of lean bacon or ham
2 onions

1 carrot
2lb potatoes
pepper and salt

Cut beef into good-sized cubes. Take all fat from mutton and also
cut into cubes. Cut bacon into one inch lengths. Slice potatoes,
carrot and onions. Put a good layer of potatoes in the bottom of a
brown earthenware dish; then a layer of meat. Season, then a layer
of onions and carrot. Season again and continue with layers of meat
and vegetables until within an inch of the top, making last layer
potatoes. Cover with water, place pan lid on top, and cook in oven
slowly for three hours. About threequarters of an hour before
serving put on a crust of good pastry, and brush over with milk.

11

Beef Steak Pudding

½lb steak

2 teaspoons flour

½ teaspoon salt

water

¼ teaspoon pepper

Pastry:

¼lb flour

¼ teaspoon baking powder

a pinch of salt

1 tablespoon crumbs

2oz suet

cold water

Cut the meat into thin pieces. Mix the flour, salt and pepper, dip the meat in the mixture, and roll up with a small piece of fat in each roll. Shred the suet and chop it finely, add to the flour, salt, baking powder, and crumbs, and mix well. Make into a stiff paste with cold water, and roll out once. Grease a half-pint basin, line it with paste, put in the meat, and add cold water to half fill it. Cover with paste, wetting the edges and pressing firmly together; trim neatly. Cover with greased paper and steam two and a half hours; or cover with cloth and boil one and a half to two hours.

North Country Steak

1lb stewing steak, cut about 1½ inches thick

1 medium sized onion, finely chopped

3 bay leaves

2 teaspoons finely chopped parsley

2oz butter

1 pint beef stock

salt and pepper to season

Mix the chopped parsley and onion. Score the steak with a sharp knife and rub the chopped parsley and onion into the cuts. Leave for an hour, season with salt and pepper and fry in the butter until well browned. Put into a casserole, heat the beef stock and add, then simmer in the oven for about two to two and a half hours. Thicken the liquid as desired.

Mutton Pudding

2lb mutton, without bone	1 onion
1 sheep's kidney, with fat	seasoning and herbs
about 8oz flour	parsley if available

Remove the fat from the kidney, chop it finely, and make a good suet crust with the fat and the flour, adding herbs and plenty of seasoning. Chop the meat and kidney into small cubes, add the chopped parsley, the onion, a little flour and plenty of seasoning. Line a greased bowl with the suet crust, pack the meat mixture into it, add stock, and put on a suet lid. Boil for two hours or steam for three.

Country women would add to this, in summer, thyme flowers and leaves, in autumn, rowan berries, in winter pickled damsons.

Jugged Hare

1 hare	2oz dripping
strained juice of small lemon	1oz butter or margarine
1oz flour	1 onion
2 cloves	12 peppercorns
small bay leaf	4 good sprigs parsley
small piece of thyme	small piece mace
salt and pepper	1½ pints good stock

Cut hare into joints, dip in flour. Brown the pieces in the dripping and place in a deep casserole. Add the onion, stuck with cloves, lemon juice, salt, pepper and stock. Put the peppercorns, parsley, thyme, bay leaf, mace into a muslin bag and add to the casserole. Cover, cook in a moderate oven for three hours. Remove the bag of herbs. Melt the butter and mix in the flour; stir this into the stock and return the casserole to the oven until the mixture thickens.

Cumberland Tatie Pot

1lb breast or neck of mutton
potatoes (quartered)
carrots (sliced)

onions
water
pepper and salt

Cut up meat, place in a flat tin. Put in next, layer of onions and a layer of carrots. Put in last, potatoes and add pepper and salt. Fill up with water. Cover with greaseproof paper and bake in a fairly hot oven for about one hour. Remove paper and brown potatoes for about half an hour.

Patterdale Special

½lb corned beef
4 large potatoes
¾lb plain flour
spice

5oz margarine
¼lb lard
a little milk
1 egg

Mix together flour, ¼lb margarine, lard and pinch salt. Add a little cold water to make a smooth paste and roll out pastry while the potatoes are cooking. Mash potatoes with remaining margarine, milk and seasoning, and mix with chopped beef. Line shallow tin with pastry. Put in corned beef and potato filling. Cover over with pastry and brush with beaten egg. Cook in moderate oven for about fifteen minutes. Sufficient for four people.

Cumberland Pork Sausages

4½lb lean pork
1½lb fat pork
¼oz sage (powdered)
(please note NO bread)

1 pinch marjoram
1oz white pepper
3oz salt

Mince through a not too fine mincer. Add other ingredients and mix well. Test flavour by cooking a little in a frying pan. Fill casings and twist into links. These sausages will keep for weeks if hung on hooks on the ceiling.

Chicken Mince

1lb cooked chicken
stick celery
1oz flour
¼ pint milk

1 onion
1oz butter
½ breakfast-cup chicken stock

Remove the meat from the bones and mince or dice finely. Finely chop onion and celery. Melt fat in a saucepan, stir in the flour and cook until quite smooth, but do not allow to colour. Gradually add the stock and milk, stirring constantly. Put in celery and onion and simmer very gently for 15 minutes. Then put in the meat. Cover the pan and remove to a very slow oven for half an hour, the heat being sufficient only to allow the chicken to become flavoured, but not to cook further. Serve in a border of mashed potatoes.

Farmhouse Chicken Casserole

1lb potatoes
seasoned flour
4 rashers diced streaky bacon
6 button or spring onions

4 chicken joints
½oz butter
2oz quartered mushrooms
½ pint chicken stock

Peel the potatoes, cut in quarters or use small new potatoes, scraped. Toss chicken joints in seasoned flour. Melt the butter in a frying pan and fry chicken until golden brown. Place in a casserole dish with the potatoes. Fry bacon, onions and mushrooms until brown and add to the casserole. Add stock to the frying pan and stir until boiling. Pour into the casserole and cover. Bake in a moderate oven, for one hour or until tender. Sprinkle with chopped parsley and serve.

SAVOURIES

Fairy Toasts

4 slices of white bread
2oz grated Cheddar cheese
½ pint milk
1½oz flour

¼lb mushrooms
1½oz butter
½ teaspoon salt

Peel and slice the mushrooms including their stalks. Melt the butter in the saucepan, add the sliced mushrooms, and cover the pan. Turn heat low and slowly sauté mushrooms until tender but not frizzled. Remove the lid, sprinkle with the flour and stir well. When blended, stir in the milk and seasoning. Simmer this thick mixture, stirring all the time, for two minutes. Meanwhile make four slices of toast, only slightly browned. Spread each slice thickly with the mixture, sprinkle with cheese and put under the grill until the cheese melts. Reserve four small mushrooms whole when cooking them and top each toast with a whole mushroom for decoration.

Potato Pancakes

Put a breakfast cup of cold mashed potatoes with 1 tablespoon flour. Add pepper and salt to season, ¼ teaspoon bicarbonate of soda and sufficient milk to make a batter. Beat well and then fry in a little hot fat until both sides are brown. Delicious served with bacon.

Cottage Cheese

1 pint of yesterday's milk
2 teaspoons lemon juice

Put the milk and lemon juice in a basin, and stir first one way and then the other. Put the vessel containing the milk into another containing cold water and place in a slow oven or over an extremely low heat until the curd separates from the whey. Pour gently into piece of butter muslin spread over colander. Tie up the corners and hang to drain. Flavour with a little salt, chopped chives or parsley.

Cheese and Onion Pie

Line a deep dish with pastry. Place on it a layer of thinly sliced onion, then one of grated cheese. Season, and place another layer of each. Then cover with pastry. Brush with milk and bake to a golden brown in a moderate oven.

Savoury Pudding (To eat with pork)

6oz suet
3 large tablespoons flour
3 teacups breadcrumbs
1 heaped teaspoon sage
   (dried)

2 eggs
1 heaped teaspoon marjoram
   (dried)
pepper and salt to taste
¼ teaspoon baking powder

Put all ingredients in a bowl. Beat in the eggs and sufficient milk to form a batter. Bake like Yorkshire pudding with dripping in the tin.

17

HOT AND COLD SWEETS

Patterdale Pudding

4oz flour
4oz sugar
3oz butter

salt
1 teaspoon baking powder
2 tablespoons milk
2 eggs

Cream butter and sugar, then add beaten eggs and flour. A few apples may be added. Steam for forty minutes and serve with white sauce or custard.

Hazelnut Pear Pie

Pastry:
6oz plain flour
3oz butter
2 egg yolks blended with
 1 tablespoon water

¼ level teaspoon salt
2oz castor sugar
3oz hazelnuts, finely ground

Filling:
¾lb firm dessert pears, peeled, cored and sliced
5oz carton single or double cream
2oz castor sugar
1 teaspoon lemon juice
Decoration: double cream, whipped

Sift together flour and salt. Rub in butter until mixture resembles fine breadcrumbs. Mix in sugar and ground nuts. Mix to form a soft dough with egg yolks and water. Chill for 10 minutes. Reserve one quarter of pastry for the lid, roll out remaining pastry and use to line an 8in. flan ring. Roll out pastry for lid into an 8in. circle and cut a 3in. circle out of centre.

Filling: Mix sliced pears with sugar and lemon juice and arrange in lined flan ring. Pour over cream.

Cumberland Pudding (1)

Mix together in a basin:

6oz breadcrumbs   4oz beef suet
4oz sugar   1 tablespoon treacle
6oz sour apples (grated)   grated rind of lemon
1/4 teaspoon mixed spice   1 teaspoon baking powder

Bind together with two eggs beaten up with half teacup milk. Turn into greased mould. Cover with greased paper. Tie with cloth and steam for two hours. It is delicious served with rum sauce.

Cumberland Pudding (2)

Place in a basin two ounces each of flour and sugar. Add an ounce of butter and the grated rind of a lemon. Sprinkle in a pinch of salt, and stand the basin before the fire until the butter melts, when it may be mixed well with a wooden spoon. Pour in a little milk, and stir thoroughly. When the mixture is quite smooth the rest of the milk may be added gradually. Leave until almost cold, then add two well-beaten eggs. and bake in a buttered dish for an hour in a moderate oven.

Cumberland Apple Pudding

1/2lb self-raising flour   1 teaspoon ground ginger
1/4lb butter (or margarine)   a pinch salt
1/4lb soft brown sugar   stewed apples

Rub in butter and mix all other dry ingredients together. Spread the dry mixture over a threequarters filled dish of the stewed apples and bake in a moderate oven until golden brown. Serve with fresh cream or custard sauce.

Summer Fruit Pudding

1½lb berries, such as blackberries, raspberries, redcurrants, etc
4 tablespoons water
4oz sugar
6-8 slices day-old bread

Heat fresh fruit in about 4 tablespoons water and 4oz sugar. Bring just to the boil. Remove crusts from bread and cut into strips. Line a 2-pint basin with bread. Fill basin with fruit, layered with remainder of bread. Put a saucer on top (it must fit into basin top) and press down with something heavy, a large stone or a pile of weights. Leave overnight in a cool place. Turn out and serve with cream.

Monday's Pudding

Mix to a batter in a basin:

4oz self-raising flour	pinch of salt
2oz suet	milk

Grease a basin and put half the batter in. Then include as much jam as you wish, and the remainder of the batter on top. Steam for two hours and serve with custard or white sauce.

Coniston Pudding

6oz short crust pastry	1oz raisins
1oz currants	½oz candied peel
1 egg	¼ pint milk
1 dessertspoon sugar	a little grated nutmeg

Line a flat enamel dish with pastry and decorate the edges. Beat up the egg, add the sugar and nutmeg, then the milk (which should be hot). Chop the peel and raisins rather coarsely, add these with the currants to the custard and pour into the prepared dish. Bake in a moderate oven for 50 minutes.

BREAD AND SCONES

Farmhouse Teacakes

Batter:
2oz plain flour
1oz melted butter or lard
⅛ pint warm milk
¼oz fresh yeast or ½ teaspoon dried yeast
Additional:

6oz plain flour	1oz sultanas
1oz castor sugar	1oz currants
⅛ pint warm milk	½oz candied peel
milk for brushing	

Blend the batter ingredients together in a mixing bowl and leave for
20 minutes until the batter is frothy. Add the additional ingredients
and mix well. Knead the dough thoroughly for about 10 minutes on
a lightly floured board. Put the dough to rise until it springs back
when pressed gently with a floured finger. (About one hour at
average room temperature). Knead the dough once again and then
shape into a ball. Flatten with rolling pin to approximately 8 inches
across and ½-inch thick. Put on a greased and floured tray and
slash with a sharp knife into eight equal sections. Brush tops with
milk. Rise until dough feels springy (about 30 minutes in a warm
place or an hour at room temperature). Brush top again with milk.
Bake towards top of a fairly hot oven for 15 to 20 minutes. Cool on
a wire tray.

Fruit Loaf (no eggs or fat)

4oz flour
4oz wholemeal flour, or 8oz
    of either
2oz sugar
3oz raisins
2oz chopped peel

1 teaspoon baking soda
½ gill milk
2 dessertspoons treacle
3oz currants
pinch salt
2 dessertspoons vinegar

Mix all the dry ingredients and add milk. Add treacle and mix well, add the vinegar last. Turn into greased tin and bake in a moderate oven for an hour.

Westmorland Buttermilk Scones

8oz flour
3oz butter
3oz sugar

¼ teaspoon salt
½ teaspoon bicarbonate of soda
½ pint buttermilk

Mix the dry ingredients together by rubbing in the butter. Dissolve soda in the milk. Mix to a soft dough and bake in hot oven for thirty minutes, turning them over after ten minutes.

Sticky Bread

2 teacups self-raising flour
4oz raisins
1 level teaspoonful bi-carb. soda

2 tablespoons sugar
2 tablespoons syrup
1 cup of milk and water

Warm the syrup, dissolve bi-carb. soda in the milk and water and add to the warm syrup. Mix the dry ingredients and stir in the liquid ingredients. When well-blended place in a greased loaf tin and bake in a slow oven for about an hour.

Nut Bread

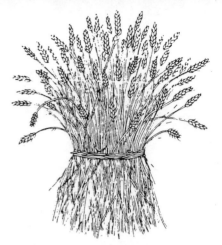

½lb self-raising flour
1 egg
a little milk
3oz margarine
2oz walnuts

Rub fat into flour. Add chopped nuts and beaten egg and milk, and make into a stiff dough. Put in greased tin and bake for half an hour in a moderate oven.

Crunchy Top Yeast Cake

8oz plain flour
2oz sugar
1oz fresh yeast or 1 level table-
    spoon dried yeast (½oz)
⅛ pint milk (5 tablespoons)
2 to 3 tablespoons jam
Topping:
2oz butter or margarine
2oz sugar

2oz fine semolina
3oz margarine
grated rind of an orange
2 eggs
2oz currants

2oz plain flour
2 rounded teaspoons cinnamon

Sieve or mix dry ingredients into a basin. Rub in fat followed by yeast. Add beaten eggs and milk, using a wooden spoon, to make a soft dough. Mix in orange rind and currants. Turn into a greased and floured shallow baking tin, 8½"×5½", and spread evenly with wet fingers. Spread jam thinly over top of cake. Rub topping ingredients lightly together to form a crumble and sprinkle over jam. Put to rise to double in size in a warm place (about 30 minutes). Bake in a fairly hot oven near the top, for 30 to 40 minutes. Turn out and cool on a wire tray.

    Delicious served buttered when very fresh, or toasted.

Wheatmeal Spoon Scones

10oz wholemeal flour
6oz plain flour
1 level teaspoon salt
2oz granulated sugar
1 level teaspoon bicarb. of soda

2 level teaspoons cream
 of tartar
2oz margarine
1 tablespoon black treacle
rather less than ½ pint
 milk

Sieve together the plain flour, salt, sugar, bicarbonate of soda and cream of tartar. Blend in the wholemeal flour. Rub in the fat. Mix the treacle and milk and stir into the flour, mixing with a round-topped knife to a heavy dropping consistency. Drop spoonfuls of the mix on to a greased oven tray (wholemeal flour). Brush lightly with milk. Bake towards the top of a hot oven for about fifteen minutes. Serve freshly baked with butter.

A COLLECTION OF CAKES

Cumberland Elderberry Cake

elderberries
sugar
½lb short crust pastry

Roll out the pastry and line a pie plate. Fill with elderberries and sugar to taste, cover with pastry and bake in a hot oven. When cool spread with a very thin layer of white icing.

Ennerdale Cake

10oz flour
6oz castor sugar
6oz butter
6oz lard

1 teaspoon baking powder
1 egg
raspberry jam
a pinch of salt

Mix like shortbread. Roll half and place in a tin. Spread jam. Roll second half and place on top. Bake for one hour in moderate oven.

Border Short Cake

4oz sugar
8oz butter or margarine
12oz plain flour

Cream butter and sugar. Add flour and work well together. Flatten out with hands about a quarter of an inch thick. Cut into fingers, place on flat greased tin, prick with fork and bake rather slowly until slightly brown. Dust with sugar while hot.

Kidsty Pike Cake

1 cup sugar
1 cup butter
2 cups flour (plain)
½ cup milk and water (warm)

2 eggs
½ teaspoon bicarbonate of
    soda
1 teaspoon cream of tartar

Cream butter and sugar. Add eggs beating the mixture well, then add milk and water and, lastly, flour with soda and tartar mixed in. Place mixture in a shallow tin. Bake in a moderate oven for about half an hour. When cold, ice the cake with the following icing: quarter cup milk; 1 cup icing sugar; threequarters cup coconut. Put milk and sugar into a pan and bring to the boil. Then pour into basin and add coconut. Stir briskly. When new milk is warm pour over Kidsty Cake.

Shap Rocks (makes 12 to 14 buns)

½lb plain flour
1 teaspoon baking powder
3oz margarine

3oz sugar
1 egg and a little milk

Rub fat into flour to which baking powder has been added; add sugar, liquid and any of the following: 1 tablespoon currants, coconut, caraway seeds or teaspoon ground ginger. Place in heaps on greased baking sheet and bake in a moderate oven fifteen to twenty minutes.

Hawkshead Cake

1¾lb flour
3oz yeast
4oz sultanas
½lb soft brown sugar
1½ level teaspoons baking
   powder

¾lb margarine
1lb currants
2oz candied peel
pinch salt
¾ pint warm (not hot) milk

Rub in the yeast, dry. Mix together the flour, sugar and salt. Rub in the fat, mix in the fruit, then mix with the warm milk. Put into well-greased tins and allow to rise in a warm place for half an hour before baking in a moderate oven about 30 to 40 minutes.

Mountain Cake

1 cup sugar
1 cup butter
½ cup warm water and milk

2 eggs
2 cups flour
1½ teaspoons baking powder

Beat butter and sugar to a cream. Add eggs, flour and milk, and lastly baking powder. Bake in a flat tin in a moderate oven for about half an hour.

Cumberland Cake

1lb flour
½lb candied peel (lemon)
2 tablespoons marmalade
1 teaspoon bicarbonate soda

¼lb raisins
6oz margarine
4oz sugar
1 small cup milk (buttermilk if obtainable)

Rub fat into flour, add dry ingredients. Dissolve soda in milk, add to other ingredients, and mix well. Put in a well greased cake tin. Bake for one and a half hours in a moderate oven.

Cumberland Sandcake

2oz butter
4oz castor sugar
4oz cornflour

1oz plain flour
1 teaspoon baking powder
2 eggs and a little lemon essence

Cream butter and sugar. Add well beaten eggs and then stir in both flours and baking powder. Mix well; add lemon essence. Put in a 7 inch prepared cake tin, bake in a moderate oven for about thirty minutes.

Rich Windermere Fruit Cake

8oz flour, plain or self-raising
½ teaspoon spice
6oz soft brown sugar
8oz currants
2oz chopped candied peel
2oz blanched chopped almonds

¼ teaspoon salt
6oz butter
4 eggs
6oz sultanas
2oz glacé cherries

Beat margarine and sugar until light and fluffy. Add the beaten eggs, one at a time, then gradually add the flour and fruit. Place in a tin lined with greased paper and bake in a moderate oven for half-an-hour, then reduce the oven to slow and bake a further two hours or until the cake remains firm when lightly pressed with a knife.

Lakeland Ginger Bread

½lb flour
4oz brown sugar
4oz butter

1 teaspoon ground ginger
1 teaspoon baking powder
1 pinch of salt

Put dry ingredients into a bowl and rub in butter very thoroughly. Spread evenly on a shallow greased tin and bake in a moderate oven for half an hour.

Dalton Gingerbread

Three cups plain flour
¼lb lard
1 cup sugar
1 cup old-fashioned dark
    treacle
1 cup boiling water

a pinch of salt
1½ teaspoons baking powder
1 teaspoon bicarbonate of soda
2 teaspoons ginger

Rub lard into flour. Mix in all the dry ingredients except bicarbonate of soda (leaving baking powder to last). Then put in the melted treacle. Mix bicarbonate of soda with boiling water and stir into the mixture. Bake in a deep roasting tin for half an hour in a moderate oven.

Kendal Ginger Cake

3oz flour
3oz cornflour or ground rice
4oz butter
2oz sugar
1oz candied peel, or grated
    rind of half a lemon

1 teaspoon ground ginger
1/4 teaspoon baking powder
yolk of one egg
1 tablespoon milk

Mix the flour, cornflour and baking powder in a bowl. Rub in the butter thoroughly, and then add sugar, ground ginger and candied peel (cut finely). Mix well together and make into a stiff paste with yolk and milk (beaten together). Roll out about a quarter of an inch thick and cut into fingers. Place on a baking tin and bake in a moderately quick oven for about ten minutes, until slightly brown. When cold, cover with a little icing or put together with jam between and ice over.

Grasmere Gingerbread Cake

4oz butter
3 eggs
1 teaspoon baking powder
3oz preserved ginger
a little grated lemon

4oz sugar
10oz plain flour
1/4 teaspoon ground ginger
1 tablespoon syrup from
    preserved ginger

Beat the butter and sugar to a cream, add each egg separately and beat thoroughly, Stir in flour, baking powder and ground ginger. Cut preserved ginger into small squares and add to the mixture with the syrup and lemon rind. Pour into tin lined with greased paper. Bake 1 3/4 hours in a slow oven.

Millom Yo-Yo's

6oz self-raising flour
3oz margarine
3oz sugar

1 beaten egg
1 good tablespoon chocolate
    powder

Cream sugar, margarine and chocolate powder. Stir in egg and flour. Form into small balls and bake in a moderate oven for twenty minutes on greased tray. Sandwich together in pairs with buttercream. Decorate with chocolate icing and shelled walnut.

Westmorland Pepper Cake

2lb flour	½oz clove pepper
1lb sugar	1oz ginger
1lb treacle	½ teaspoon black pepper
½lb butter	2 teaspoons baking powder
½lb currants	2oz candied lemon
½lb Valencia raisins	3 eggs

Rub butter into flour, add fruit and spice, and mix with treacle and eggs. Put into a well-greased cake tin. Bake in a slow oven.

Cumberland Soda Cake

1lb flour	½lb sultanas
½lb sugar	½lb margarine
½lb currants	1oz candied peel
2 teaspoons bi-carb soda	pinch salt

Rub fat in flour and mix rest of ingredients, except bicarbonate of soda. Dissolve in 2 tablespoonsful of milk and mix all together. Stand overnight. Put into a greased cake tin. Bake in a slow oven next morning for two hours.

Derwent Queen of Hearts

8oz self-raising flour	1 large egg
4oz margarine	a little milk
4oz sugar	a pinch of salt
2oz mixed dried fruit	

Cream together margarine and sugar, add half quantity of flour with little of beaten egg, and pinch of salt. Add rest of flour, fruit and remaining egg. Stir together, adding little milk until soft dropping mixture. Put into greased bun tins or paper cases. Place in a medium oven for twenty minutes.

Shortbread

5oz flour
1oz ground rice
4oz butter
2oz castor sugar

Beat butter and sugar together. Add flour and knead well. Roll about a quarter of an inch thick and place on a greased flat tin. Leave the mixture to stand an hour or so before cooking in a moderate oven. Cut when still warm.

Ulverston Shortbread or Meg's Shortbread

2oz icing sugar
6oz self-raising flour
4oz margarine

Blend the icing sugar and flour, rub in the fat to form a dough (no liquid should be used). Roll out about ½ inch thick, cut into rounds and place on a greased baking sheet. Bake in a moderate oven until golden brown.

Chocolate Shortcake

1 cup flour
4oz margarine
1 cup coconut
1 tablespoon cocoa

Mix the dry ingredients, rub in the fat until the mixture is crumbly. Press into a well-greased, oblong tin and bake in a moderate oven about 20 minutes. When baked make a chocolate icing and spread over the shortbread while still hot.

Coffee and Cinnamon Cakes

8oz plain flour
1oz castor sugar
2½oz butter or margarine
Filling:
Castor sugar as required
1½oz butter or margarine

1 level teaspoon baking powder
milk to mix flavoured well
with coffee

1 level teaspoon cinnamon
2oz sultanas
Coffee syrup

Sieve flour and baking powder and mix in sugar. Rub in fat finely, then mix to a soft but not sticky dough with the coffee-flavoured milk. Knead lightly for a moment to make smooth, then roll out about ¼ inch thick to an oblong about 10 inches by 8 inches. Brush a little coffee syrup over surface of dough – sparingly. Then sprinkle with castor sugar, mixed with cinnamon. Melt fat without oiling and brush over dough within an inch of the edges. Sprinkle with sultanas. Moisten edges of dough then roll up and seal firmly along join. Wrap in waxed or greaseproof paper and chill in refrigerator. Cut into ¾ inch wide slices with a sharp knife and bake lying flat on a greased baking tin in a brisk oven, Mark 7 (420°F) until cakes are risen and golden brown. Dust with powdered sugar before serving.

Lardy Johns

½lb plain flour
3oz home-cured lard or bacon fat
   (if bacon fat is used omit salt)
2 oz sugar

2oz currants
a little cold water
a pinch of salt

Sieve flour and salt. Rub in lard until mixture is crumbly. Stir in sugar and currants, mix to a stiff paste with cold water. Roll out on floured board and cut into two-inch squares, place on greased baking sheet, bake for fifteen minutes in a fairly hot oven.

Biscuits Baked in Lakeland

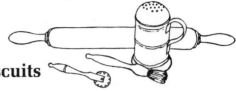

Windermere Spice Biscuits

¼lb butter
¼lb sugar
1 teaspoon caraway seeds

6oz flour
½ teaspoon cinnamon
1 large egg

Beat butter and sugar to a cream. Add the flour, caraway seeds and enough of the beaten egg to make a stiff paste. Roll out in rounds with a pastry cutter and bake for thirty minutes in a moderate oven.

Cumberland Snaps

2 cups self-raising flour
1 cup rolled oats
1 cup soft brown sugar
1 teaspoon bicarbonate of
   soda

¼lb margarine
2 tablespoons syrup
1 small teaspoon ginger
a pinch of salt

Put the margarine and syrup into a pan to melt. Mix together the flour, oats, sugar, ginger and salt. Add the soda dissolved in a little warm water, and then add the melted margarine and syrup. Mix and then roll into balls. Place on a greased baking sheet, and flatten a little with a fork. Bake in a moderate oven about fifteen minutes.

Cumberland Nickies

½lb short pastry
3oz currants
1 tablespoon Demerara sugar

½ teaspoon grated nutmeg
1oz butter
1 tablespoon rum

Melt butter, add nutmeg and rum. Now add currants and sugar. Leave to steep for an hour. Roll pastry thinly, cut into rounds, stir currant mixture well. Spread a little on one round of pastry: cover with another, prick. Bake in a hot oven for ten to fifteen minutes.

Almond Biscuits

3oz plain flour
4oz ground almonds
1 egg
a few glacé cherries

3oz castor sugar
2oz margarine
1 teaspoon almond essence

Rub margarine into flour, add sugar, ground almonds and mix well together. Beat the egg and add to the mixture along with the almond essence. Mix to a soft paste. Mould with the hands into small flat biscuits, place half a glacé cherry on top of each. Put on a greased baking sheet and bake in a moderate oven 20 to 30 minutes.

Hawkshead Biscuits

1lb self-raising flour
1oz castor sugar
1 egg, well beaten

3oz butter
a pinch of salt
½ pint milk

Rub the butter into the flour, add the sugar and salt and mix to a light dough with the beaten egg and milk. Divide into eight pieces, roll each piece out about ½ inch thick, prick all over with a fork, place on greased baking sheets and bake in a moderate oven about 15 minutes.

Nutty Dainties

4oz butter or margarine
4oz rolled oats
1½ tablespoons syrup

4oz sugar
4oz desiccated coconut

Mix all dry ingredients together, melt butter and syrup and when cool add. Place in shallow, greased tin and bake in a slow oven. Cut into fingers when cooling.

Seasonal Dishes

Shrovetide

Westmorland Cream Pancakes

Mix 8oz flour, 1 level teaspoon bicarbonate of soda, 1 level
teaspoon cream of tartar, pinch salt, ¼ pint of cream. Mix with ¼
pint milk (sour milk if possible), then the cream of tartar may be
omitted. Dissolve bicarbonate of soda and cream of tartar in the
milk and cream mixture before adding to the flour and salt. Cook in
lightly greased pan over moderate heat, turning when cooked on
one side. This makes several pancakes of average size or you can
make a larger number of small ones.

Snow Pancakes

1 heaped tablespoon flour
3 tablespoons of milk
a pinch of salt

Mix to a stiff batter. Add one tablespoon of fine powdery snow.
Again mix. Fry in available fat and serve with jam or dried fruit.
The above quantities are for one pancake. Given the right kind of
snow (not the wet, heavy variety) the results should be good.

Easter

Easter Cake

6oz flour	1oz almonds
4oz castor sugar	2 eggs
4oz butter or margarine	1 tablespoon milk
4oz sultanas	½ teaspoon baking powder
2oz mixed peel	grated rind of half a lemon

Beat butter and sugar to a cream, and then beat in eggs. Add sifted flour, fruit, peel and almonds (blanched and sliced). Fold in baking powder and lemon rind; add milk and beat well. Bake for one hour and a half in moderate oven after placing mixture in paper-lined tin. Leave cake for two days. Then ice as follows: Sieve 6oz icing sugar into a bowl, add 1 teaspoon of lemon juice, a few drops of green colouring, and enough water to form a thin paste. Spread this over cake, first fastening a paper round cake to prevent icing running down sides. Stand cake in a warm place to dry. Remove paper next day, decorate with little marzipan ducklings or other Easter novelties, making little marzipan nests, fill with tiny eggs from confectioners or make some from sugar coloured green. Surround cake with a frill of green tissue, cut finely at edges to represent grass.

Easter-ledge Pudding

Easter-ledges about 4-in high	teacup barley
half as many young nettles	½ teaspoon salt
1 large onion	

Remove stems of Easter-ledges and chop well together with young nettles and onion, wash the barley and sprinkle this in among the greens adding the salt. Put all together and tie up in a muslin bag and boil for one and a half to two hours. Before serving, beat it up in a dish with one egg and some butter (or bacon dripping is excellent) flavour well with salt and pepper.

Hot Cross Buns

1lb flour
a pinch of salt
¾oz yeast
2 tablespoons sugar
2oz margarine

2oz currants
1 level teaspoon cinnamon
1 level teaspoon mixed spice
1 egg
about ½ pint milk

Sieve flour with salt and spices, rub in fat and add currants. Cream the yeast with a little sugar, add a little warm milk and pour in centre of flour, sprinkle lightly over with flour and leave for ten minutes. Mix to a stiff dough with the beaten egg, adding a little milk if required. Allow to rise until the mixture doubles itself in size, divide into twelve portions, mould into small buns, mark with a cross and place on a greased and floured tin. Allow to rise until half as large again. Bake in a hot oven about eight minutes. Melt a little sugar in a tablespoon of milk and brush over the buns when baked.

Summertime

Clipping-Time Pudding

8oz rice
4oz currants
4oz stoned raisins
3oz sugar
1 egg

1 pint milk
a little cinnamon
2 beef marrow bones, cooked
  and marrow extracted
a little salt

Blanch the rice in a little salt water, then cool it slowly in milk. Add sugar and cinnamon and boil until tender. Beat the egg and add to the rice, together with the currants and raisins, and stir well together. Then add the marrow, cut into small pieces. Bake for twenty minutes in a moderate oven (Regulo 7).

Haymakers' Cocktail

½ pint orange juice from very sweet oranges
½ pint milk (new)

Pour the orange juice slowly on to the milk, beating it into the milk all the time to ensure a thorough mixing. NO sugar should be added. The orange greatly increases the digestibility and palatability of the milk, making the drink refreshing and at the same time sustaining.

Plot Night

Westmorland Parkin (1)

1lb medium oatmeal
½lb flour
4oz lard
4oz dripping
½lb brown sugar

½lb treacle
½oz ginger
¼oz mixed spice
½ teaspoon bicarbonate of soda and a little milk

Mix to a stiff dough, roll out and cut into rounds with a pastry cutter; place on a flat, greased baking sheet and bake in a slow oven about fifteen minutes.

Westmorland Parkin (2)

1lb fine oatmeal
½lb flour
1lb treacle
½lb butter
½lb Demerara sugar

1 teaspoon allspice
1 teaspoon salt
1 teaspoon bicarbonate of soda
2 teaspoons baking powder
½ cup milk

Put the butter in a dish in the oven to melt the treacle. Sift dry ingredients into a bowl, make a well in the centre, add the bicarbonate of soda dissolved in the milk (slightly warmed). Mix well. Grease a large, shallow meat tin. Put in the mixture. Cook in a moderate oven for one and a half hours. When cold cut into three-inch squares.

Oaty Parkins

1 cup flour
2 cups oats
1 tablespoon treacle
pinch of salt

1 cup sugar
¼lb margarine and lard mixed
1 level teaspoon bi-carb soda
1 level teaspoon ginger

Heat treacle and fat together, mix bi-carb. soda with a little hot
water and stir into the treacle and fat, add dry ingredients and mix,
adding a little more water if necessary, but do not make too soft.
Roll out on a floured board, cut into rounds with a biscuit cutter
and bake in a moderate oven, 10 to 15 minutes.

Old Fashioned Parkin

¼lb plain flour
¾ teaspoon bi-carb soda
½lb medium oatmeal
½lb brown sugar
1 egg
½ teaspoon cinnamon

1 heaped teaspoon ground
    ginger
½lb black treacle
3oz butter or margarine
5 to 6 tablespoons milk

Sieve together the flour, cinnamon, ginger and bi-carbonate of soda
and add the oatmeal. Slowly melt the butter or margarine, treacle
and sugar in a saucepan and add, with the beaten egg, to the
flour mixture. Lastly stir in the milk and mix thoroughly to form a
fairly soft batter. Turn into a square tin lined with greased
greaseproof paper and bake in a slow oven, 40 to 50 minutes. Cut,
the following day, into thick fingers or squares.

Christmas

Cumberland Sweet Pie

½lb fat mutton chops (raw) a pinch of cinnamon
½lb currants mace
½lb sultanas nutmeg
½lb raisins pepper
6oz brown sugar ¼oz teaspoon salt
juice of one large lemon 2oz mixed peel

Fill pie dish with alternate layers of the mixture, beginning with mutton. Cover with rough puff pastry. Bake in a quick oven.

Christmas Bread

1¾lb flour 1 tablespoon black treacle
3oz lard 2oz mixed peel
6oz sugar 2 eggs
4oz currants 1 teaspoon spice
8oz raisins 1 teaspoon salt
4oz sultanas 1oz yeast

Put the flour and salt into a warm bowl and stand by the fire to warm. Rub in the lard. Cream the yeast in a basin with one teaspoon of sugar. Beat the eggs well and add sufficient warm milk and water to make threequarters of a pint, including the eggs. Stir into the yeast and mix well. Make a well in the middle of the flour, and pour mixture in. Set to rise half an hour in a warm place, then knead well and add all the fruit, sugar, etc., warmed. Mix well and leave to rise for two hours; then put into two loaf tins. Rise for twenty minutes more and bake for one hour fifteen minutes in a moderate oven.

Jams, Jellies and Preserves

Apple Ginger

2lb apples   2lb loaf sugar
4oz crystallized ginger (shredded)   1½ pints water

Boil sugar and water to a syrup. Peel, core and cut apples in quarters (dip in cold water to preserve colour). Add ginger and syrup, boil until transparent. Put in jars and store in a dry place.

Apple Marmalade

Peel and core apples, slice into eights and place in basin of water. To every pound of fruit allow 1lb sugar, ¼oz whole ginger and half a lemon. Move apples from water into preserving pan and boil with sugar, lemons and ginger until quite clear — the rind of the lemon is best put in with the ginger, but juice should not be added until about twenty minutes before preserve is ready.

Vegetable Marrow Jam

For 7lb of fruit, 2lb of brown sugar boiled for one and a half hours in three gills of water.

Cut the marrow into small pieces and pour the above syrup over it while still boiling. Then add 6lb white sugar, 2oz preserved ginger (or ground ginger to taste), 12 cayenne pods and two lemons cut up finely. Boil until it is syrupy, as marrow jam does not set in a jelly.

41

Damson Jam

4lb damsons
4lb granulated sugar
a good half-pint water

Wash the damsons and allow to dry, then simmer them gently in the water until soft, remove the stones as they come to the top. Add the sugar which has been warmed in the oven, stir to dissolve it and bring to the boil. Boil moderately fast until a little will set when tested. Put into warmed jars and cover when cold.

Pickled Kendal Damsons

Prick one quart of damsons with a fine needle. Put them in the jar in which it is intended to keep them. Boil ½ pint vinegar and 1lb loaf sugar together and pour it over the damsons. Allow them to stand twenty-four hours. Pour liquid off and bring to the boil. Then pour back on to damsons. The following day boil the fruit with the vinegar and 2oz of stick cinnamon and 1oz of cloves but not long enough to burst the skins of the damsons. This pickle will be ready for use in six weeks.

Blackcurrant syrup

Wash the blackcurrants and put into a pan (stainless steel, aluminium or enamel). Do not add any more water than adheres to the fruit after washing. Bring to the boil, stirring constantly and boil for two minutes only. Strain the fruit through a jelly bag, overnight. Next day add 12oz granulated sugar to each pint of juice and stir until the sugar dissolves. Pour into screw-top bottles to within 2 inches of the top and seal. Sterilise by placing the bottles in a pan with a false bottom (slats of wood or newspaper placed in the bottom of an ordinary pan will serve quite well) and fill the pan with water up to the base of the screw cap. Heat to 170 degrees Far. and maintain for 20 minutes without boiling. Cool the bottles and store in a cool, dark place.

Marrow Cream Cheese

2lb marrow   ¼lb butter
2lb sugar   rind and juice of three lemons

Peel marrow and take out seeds. Boil until tender (or it may be steamed). Strain away all the liquid and pass the marrow through a sieve. Beat it up and place in a preservng pan with the grated lemon rind and juice. Boil until it thickens, stirring all the time. Add butter and mix ingredients together well. Put in jars and cover while hot. It will keep for months.

Keswick Jelly

1 pint milk   3 tablespoons sugar
2 eggs   ½oz gelatine

Dissolve gelatine in nearly boiling milk. Separate whites from yolks of eggs. Beat 2½ teaspoons sugar with yolks and flavour with vanilla, almond or lemon essence. Beat ½ teaspoon sugar with egg whites to a stiff froth. When gelatine has dissolved boil up the yolks in the milk, then pour the mixture on to the whisked whites. Mix together and pour into mould. The mixture sets half jelly and half creamy.

Tomato Chutney

¾lb sultanas   2lb Green tomatoes
1lb cooking apples   ½lb onions
½lb soft brown sugar   ¼ teaspoon salt
¼ teaspoon pepper   ¼ teaspoon dry mustard

Remove the skin from onions, core the apples but do not peel. Then put all the ingredients through the mincer, put into a saucepan or preserving pan, boil until stiff and bottle when cool.

Trimmings and Toffee

Cumberland Sauce

4 level tablespoons redcurrant jelly
1 level teaspoon made mustard
2 tablespoons port wine or elderberry wine
rind of 1 lemon finely sliced and boiled until
    tender

Mix well together the redcurrant jelly, wine and mustard, add the cooked lemon rind and stir in. May be served hot or cold.

Clear Lemon Sauce

1 pint water
2 tablespoons sugar

2 tablespoons cornflour
1 lemon

Put the water on to boil, then add cornflour and sugar mixed to a paste with cold water, mix in grated rind and juice of lemon and boil for five minutes. Serve hot.

Fudge

1lb soft brown sugar
1 cup chopped walnuts
a piece of butter the size of a walnut.

Put all the ingredients into a saucepan over low heat and stir until the sugar has dissolved, bring slowly to the boil and boil for three minutes, stirring gently all the time. Remove from heat and beat until the mixture is thick. Pour into tins previously greased with butter and cut into squares when cold.

Cumberland Butter

¼lb fresh butter
1lb soft brown sugar

nutmeg and mixed spice to taste
¾ wineglass rum

Melt ¼lb of fresh butter, and then add other ingredients. Mix thoroughly. Place it in a pretty bowl and sift sugar over it.

Ambleside Toffee

2lb white sugar
½ a large tin condensed milk
a pinch of salt

¼lb butter
1 teacup water

Put all the ingredients in a strong pan, stir over gentle heat, taking care it does not burn. When toffee begins to thicken, take off heat and stir for one minute, add a few drops of vanilla essence. Pour into a well-buttered tin and when cold mark off into squares.

Mock Cream

Half a cup of milk
1 tablespoon butter
vanilla essence to taste

1 dessertspoon cornflour
1 tablespoon sugar

Beat to a cream the butter and sugar. Mix the cornflour with a little of the milk, boil the rest of the milk and stir into the cornflour, then return to pan and boil for one minute. Allow to cool. Add to the creamed butter and sugar, flavour with vanilla essence.

Drinks

Blackberry Cordial (Kendal)

5lb blackberries (or other fruit)   1 quart cold water
2¼oz citric acid   1½lb lump sugar

Let blackberries, water and citric acid stand for 24 hours. Strain and add 1½lb lump sugar to 1 pint of juice. Let it stand 24 hours stirring well several times. Bottle and seal. It will keep for years.

Elder Flower Champagne

2 handfuls flowers minus stalks juice and rind of one lemon
1 gallon water   2 tablespoons white wine
1½lb granulated sugar   vinegar

Put all ingredients into a vessel and stir them together. Let them stand for 24 hours. Strain and bottle. The champagne will be ready for drinking in a few days.

Broughton Ginger Wine

3oz root ginger (bruised)   ½oz cream of tartar
2 sliced lemons   2 gallons boiling water
2lb lump sugar   ½oz yeast

Pour boiling water over all ingredients except yeast. When tepid place yeast on top. Allow to stand for 2 days. Skim and strain, bottle and cork tightly.

Nettle Tops

2 gallons young nettle tops
2oz hops
½oz root ginger
4oz malt

4oz sarsaparilla root (these can
    be bought from a chemist)
1½lb castor sugar
2 gallons water
1oz yeast

Wash the nettles, bruise the ginger and slice the sarsaparilla thinly. Put them into a large saucepan with the malt and hops, add the water and bring gently to the boil. Boil for half-hour. Put the sugar into a pan, strain the liquid on to it and stir in till the sugar is dissolved. Dissolve the yeast in a cupful of the warm liquid and add it to the pan when the contents of it are cool. Let it stand for three days covered with muslin. Stir daily. Then bottle off or put it into a large stone jar, leaving corks loose until fermentation has ceased. Then cork and tie corks down with string.

Metric Equivalents

¼oz	7g	1lb	454g
½oz	14g	2lb	907g
¾oz	21g	3lb	1.36kg
1oz	28g		
4oz (¼lb)	113g	¼ pint (1 gill)	142ml
8oz (½lb)	227g	½ pint	283ml
12oz (¾lb)	340g	1 pint	576ml